Insta-Success: Building Your Brand and Growing Your Business on Instagram

B. Vincent

Published by RWG Publishing, 2023.

While every precaution has been taken in the preparation of this book, the publisher assumes no responsibility for errors or omissions, or for damages resulting from the use of the information contained herein.

INSTA-SUCCESS: BUILDING YOUR BRAND AND GROWING YOUR BUSINESS ON INSTAGRAM

First edition. May 7, 2023.

Copyright © 2023 B. Vincent.

Written by B. Vincent.

Also by B. Vincent

Business Bogging
Business Communication Course
Marketing Automation
Better Meetings
Business Conflict Resolution
Business Culture Course
Conversion Optimization
Creative Solutions
Employee Recruitment
Startup Capital
Employee Incentives
Employee Mentoring
Followership
Servant Leadership
Human Resources
Team Building
Freelancing
Funnel Building
Geo Targeting
Goal Setting
Immanent List Building
Lead Generation
Leadership Course
Leadership Transition
Leadership vs Management
LinkedIn Ads
LinkedIn Marketing
Messenger Marketing
New Management
Newsfeed Ads
Search Ads
Online Learning
Sales Webinars

Side Hustles

Split Testing

Twitter Timeline Advertising

Earning Additional Income Through Side Hustles: Begin Earning Money Immediately

Making a Living Through Blogging: Earn Money Working From Home

Create Bonuses for Affiliate Marketing: Your Success Is Encompassed by Your Bonuses

Internet Marketing Success: The Most Effective Traffic-Driving Strategies

JV Recruiting: Joint Ventures Partnerships and Affiliates

Secrets to List Building

Step-by-Step Facebook Marketing: Discover How To Create A Strategy That Will Help You Grow Your Business

Banner Advertising: Traffic Can Be Boosted by Banner Ads

Affiliate Marketing

Improve Your Marketing Strategy with Internet Marketing

Outsourcing Helps You Save Time and Money

Choosing the Right Content and Marketing for Social Media

Make Products That Will Sell

Launching a Product for Affiliate Marketing

Pinterest as a Marketing Tool

Banner Blitz: Mastering the Art of Advertising with Eye-Catching Banners

Beyond Commissions: Maximizing Affiliate Profits with Creative Bonus Strategies

Retargeting Mastery: Winning Sales with Online Strategies

Power Partnerships: Mastering the Art of Business Growth Through Partnership Recruiting

The List Advantage: Unlocking the Power of List Building for Marketing Success

Capital Catalyst: The Essential Guide to Raising Funds for Your Business
Mobile Mastery: The Ultimate Guide to Successful Mobile Marketing Campaigns
Crowdfunding Secrets: A Comprehensive Guide to Successfully Funding Your Next Project
Insta-Success: Building Your Brand and Growing Your Business on Instagram

Table of Contents

Chapter 1: Introduction - Why Instagram is the Ultimate Platform for Business Success

———

With more than one billion active users on a monthly basis, Instagram has quickly emerged as one of the most popular social media platforms available worldwide. Because it is a platform that is primarily visual and is designed to share photos and videos, it is an excellent choice for companies that want to demonstrate their goods and services to potential customers. We are going to go over the many reasons why Instagram is the best platform for a successful business in this chapter.

Instagram's User Base

As was just mentioned, Instagram has more than 1 billion active users on a monthly basis, with over 500 million using the platform on a daily basis. Because of the large number of users, businesses have access to a massive potential audience with which they can connect and market their products and services. Over seventy-one percent of Instagram's user base is comprised of users who are younger than 35 years old. These users are highly engaged. Because of this, businesses that are interested in reaching younger demographics will find Instagram to be an ideal platform.

Instagram's Visual Nature

Photos and videos are the most common forms of content that are uploaded and shared on Instagram due to the platform's emphasis on visual storytelling. Due to the visual nature of the platform, it is an excellent choice for companies that want to showcase the products or services they offer. Businesses can give their audience a glimpse into what they offer by sharing images and videos of high quality, which can create a desire in the audience to make a purchase or learn more about the business.

Instagram's Engagement

Users spend an average of 53 minutes per day using the Instagram app, indicating that the platform provides a high level of user engagement. Because of the high level of engagement, companies now have the chance to connect with their target audience and establish new relationships with them. Businesses are able to maintain their followers' engagement and interest in their brand by consistently posting new content.

The Algorithm Behind Instagram

Because the Instagram algorithm chooses the content that users see in their feeds, it is critical for businesses to have a solid understanding of how the algorithm operates. The algorithm takes into account a number of different factors, such as engagement, relevancy, and timeliness, among others. Businesses can optimize their content and increase the likelihood that it will appear on the feeds of their followers by first gaining an understanding of how the algorithm operates.

The Functions of Instagram

Instagram provides its users with a variety of features that can be utilized to the benefit of their businesses. Engaging with one's audience on Instagram can be done in a variety of ways, from Instagram Stories to Instagram Live, and businesses have access to all of these features. Instagram also provides businesses with a number of advertising options, enabling them to tailor their messages to the demographics and interests of a particular audience.

The Influence That Instagram Has on Sales

Businesses can expect to see a significant increase in sales after utilizing Instagram. According to Instagram, over 200 million users of the platform visit at least one business profile every single day, and 60 percent of these users learn about new products through the platform. In addition, thirty percent of people who use Instagram have bought products that they found for the first time on the platform.

Conclusion

In conclusion, Instagram is the best platform for commercial success due to the large number of highly engaged users it has, the visual nature of its content, the engagement it encourages, the algorithm it uses, the features it offers, and the impact it has on sales. Businesses that are able to connect with their target audience on Instagram, develop meaningful relationships with customers, and ultimately increase sales are the most successful users of the platform. In the following chapter, we will go over how to define your brand identity on Instagram as well as how to set goals for your account.

Chapter 2: Setting Goals and Defining Your Brand Identity on Instagram

———

It is important to establish crystal clear goals and clearly define your brand identity before you can begin developing your brand on Instagram and expanding your business using the platform. In this chapter, we'll go over how to define your brand identity on Instagram as well as how to set goals for your account there.

Establishing Objectives on Instagram

The first thing you need to do to build a successful strategy for Instagram is to establish your goals. Your objectives ought to be particular, measurable, reachable, pertinent, and constrained by a time frame. The following is a list of some examples of goals that you could set for yourself on Instagram:

Within the next half a year, bring your total number of followers up by 20%.

You can drive more traffic to your website by increasing the number of clicks on the link in your Instagram bio by fifty percent within the next three months.

Within the next three months, you should aim to achieve a 25% increase in engagement.

Within the next year, you should be able to generate $10,000 in sales from Instagram.

Establishing the Identity of Your Brand on Instagram

Defining the personality of your company or product is another important step in developing a winning strategy for Instagram. Your audience will be able to connect with you on a deeper level and be differentiated from your competitors thanks to your brand identity, which is what sets you apart from them. The following are some steps that will assist you in defining the identity of your brand on Instagram:

Define your mission statement

Your brand's purpose and the values you uphold should be outlined in a statement that is both clear and succinct, and this statement should serve as your mission statement. Additionally, it should be in line with the objectives of your company. Your mission statement ought to be reflected in every aspect of your Instagram strategy, from your bio to your posts, and it ought to be clear to anyone who views your profile.

Identify your target audience

It is essential to have a solid understanding of your target audience in order to produce content that will resonate with them. You need to develop a buyer persona that outlines the demographic and psychographic characteristics of your target audience, such as their age, gender, interests, and pain points. This can be accomplished by creating a buyer persona document.

Establish the voice and tone of your brand.

The personality and ideals of your company should come through in the voice and tone of your brand. It ought to be consistent across the entirety of the content you post to Instagram, from your captions to your stories. Your target demographic should be able to identify with the voice and attitude of your brand.

Develop a style guide for the company brand.

A document that outlines your brand's visual identity, including your brand colors, typography, and imagery, is called a brand style guide. Your audience will have an easier time recognizing your brand if the visual identity of your brand is maintained consistently across all of your Instagram content.

Find out what your content strategy is.

It is important that the goals of your company, its mission statement, and its brand identity all align with your content strategy. It is also important to think about the people who are going to be reading the content, as well as the kinds of things that will resonate with them. Your content strategy should include the categories of content that you will post, the number of times per week that you will post, and the topics that you will discuss.

Conclusion

It is essential to the development of a successful Instagram strategy to establish crystal clear goals and to define the identity of your brand on Instagram. Your objectives ought to be particular, measurable, reachable, pertinent, and constrained by a time frame. Your brand identity should be consistent across all of your Instagram content, and it should reflect your brand's purpose, personality, and values. Additionally, your brand identity should be reflected in your brand's name. In the following section, we will talk about how to create the ideal Instagram profile for yourself.

Chapter 3: Crafting the Perfect Instagram Profile: Tips and Tricks

―――

When users navigate to your page on Instagram, the very first thing they will see is your profile. It is extremely important to create a positive first impression and grab the attention of your audience right away. In this section, we will go over some pointers and strategies that can help you craft the ideal Instagram profile.

Pick a picture for your profile that accurately reflects your company.

One of the most important aspects of your Instagram profile is the picture that you use as your profile picture. When users visit your page, it is the very first thing that they see on the screen. Pick a picture for your profile that accurately reflects your company, such as a high-quality picture of one of your products or your company's logo.

Write a compelling bio

Your audience has the opportunity to learn more about who you are and what you do through your bio. It ought to be concise, unmistakable, and persuasive. Make use of keywords that are associated with your brand, and don't forget to incorporate a call to action that inspires users to interact with the content you provide.

Create a user name that's easy to remember.

Your username ought to be easily recognizable and should convey some aspect of your brand. You should try to keep your username free of any numbers or special characters. If it's at all possible, use the name of your company as your username.

Include a link to your website in the response.

You are allowed to include one link that users can click on within your Instagram bio. Users can be directed to your website, online store, or a specific landing page by using this link. You can use software such as Linktree or Lnk if you want to incorporate more than one link into your post.Bio.

Put the spotlight on your most valuable content.

Using the "Highlights" feature of Instagram, you are able to call attention to the content that you feel is particularly noteworthy within your profile. With the help of this feature, you'll be able to save and organize your Stories into a variety of highlight reels. Make the most of this function to display your most compelling content and provide users with a clearer picture of what your company stands for.

Pick a motif to serve as the basis for your profile.

Your brand should be reflected in the theme that you use on your Instagram profile, and it should be consistent. Pick a color scheme, and stay consistent with it. In order to keep the look and feel of your photos and videos consistent with one another, use the same filters and editing techniques for both types of media.

Highlights should be optimized for your Instagram Story.

The highlights feature on Instagram Stories is a powerful tool that can be used to showcase your brand and engage your audience. Select highlight covers that are congruent with your company's image, and be sure to incorporate keywords into your titles. You can also include hashtags and additional information about your brand by using the highlight descriptions.

Utilize Instagram Insights to enhance the performance of your profile.

Instagram Insights gives you access to useful information regarding your audience and how they engage with the content you post. Make use of this information to improve your profile and produce content that speaks to your audience on a deeper level. For instance, if you find that your audience interacts with video content more often, you might want to concentrate on producing more video content for your profile.

Conclusion

Creating the ideal Instagram profile is essential if you want to attract the attention of your target demographic and establish a strong presence for your brand on the platform. Use a high-quality profile picture, write a compelling bio, select a memorable username, include a link to your website, highlight your best content, select a theme for your profile, optimize your Instagram Story highlights, and use Instagram Insights to optimize your profile. All of these things will help you get the most out of your Instagram presence. In the following section, we will talk about how to make captivating visual and video content for your Instagram profile, so stay tuned for that!

Chapter 4: Captivating Your Audience with Eye-Catching Visuals and Videos

---

Instagram is built on the foundation of aesthetically pleasing content. You need to produce visually appealing content and videos that engage your audience if you want to grow your business on the platform and build your brand at the same time. In this chapter, we will discuss some tips and tricks for creating captivating visual and video content for your Instagram profile. This content can include both photos and videos.

Make use of images of a high quality.

When it comes to producing visually appealing content on Instagram, having high-quality images is absolutely necessary. Take pictures with a smartphone or camera that is of a high quality to get shots that have vivid colors and clear details. You can also enhance your photographs and give them a one-of-a-kind appearance by editing them with software such as Adobe Lightroom or VSCO.

Put your brand on display with the help of some videos.

Videos are an effective medium to demonstrate your company's wares and to engage your target audience. Make use of videos to provide your audience with a glimpse of what goes on behind the scenes at your company, demonstrate how your products are used, or tell an engaging story. When editing your videos, you can add music, text, or special effects by using editing software such as Adobe Premiere Pro or Apple's iMovie.

Use Instagram filters

Instagram provides a number of different filters that you can apply to your photos and videos in order to enhance their appearance. Experiment with a variety of filters to determine which ones best capture the essence of your company and ring true with your target demographic. You can also create your own personalized filters by employing image editing software such as Lightroom or VSCO.

Integrate your brand into the visuals you create.

Include your company's branding in the images you post to Instagram in order to give your profile a more unified appearance and feel. For the purpose of reinforcing your brand identity with your visuals, use the colors, fonts, and logos associated with your brand. Canva and Adobe Spark are two examples of tools that can be used to create branded templates for your Instagram Stories.

Make use of captions so that you can tell a story.

Your Instagram posts won't be complete without accompanying captions. You can tell a story, share insights, or ask questions through the use of captions. Make your content discoverable to new audiences by utilizing keywords and hashtags in your posts. Emojis are another way to inject personality and humor into the captions of your photos and videos.

Create content that will keep people interested by using Instagram Stories.

The use of Instagram Stories is an effective method for developing engaging content that can be shared on Instagram. You can run polls, quizzes, or showcase user-generated content by using Instagram Stories. You can also use Instagram Stories to share behind-the-scenes looks at your business. You can increase the appeal of your Stories by utilizing features such as stickers, GIFs, and music.

Explore a variety of presentation methods.

Experiment with a variety of formats to maintain the uniqueness and interest of your content. You can keep your audience interested in what you have to say by mixing up your content and posting it in a variety of formats, such as Instagram Reels, IGTV videos, and carousel posts.

Utilize Instagram Analytics to fine-tune the content you post.

Instagram Analytics provides you with useful information regarding the ways in which your audience engages with the content you post. Make use of this data to optimize your content and produce visuals and videos that are more interesting to your audience. If you find that your audience interacts with videos more than images, for instance, you might want to concentrate on producing more video content for your profile.

Conclusion

In order to successfully build your brand and engage your audience on Instagram, the production of visually appealing content and videos is essential. Use images, videos, and Instagram filters of a high quality; incorporate your brand into your visuals; use captions to tell a story; use Instagram Stories to create content that is engaging; experiment with various formats; and use Instagram Analytics to optimize your content. In the following chapter, we will go over how to make use of Instagram's Storytelling feature in order to build your brand on the platform.

Chapter 5: Instagram Storytelling: How to Use Stories to Build Your Brand

Building your brand on Instagram can be accomplished with the help of the powerful tool that is Instagram Stories. Instagram Stories gives businesses the opportunity to connect with their audience and increase brand awareness, and the platform has more than 500 million daily users who are actively using it. In this chapter, we'll go over how to build your brand on Instagram by making use of the Instagram Storytelling feature.

Telling stories on Instagram is a great way to highlight the personality of your brand.

With Instagram Storytelling, businesses have the opportunity to demonstrate the personality of their brand and establish a more personal connection with their audience. You can use Instagram Stories to share glimpses of what goes on behind the scenes of your company, highlight your employees, or showcase your company's culture. Your audience will find it easier to connect with your brand and develop trust if you do this.

Make use of the Storytelling feature on Instagram to draw attention to your goods or offerings.

The Instagram Stories feature is an excellent tool for generating sales by drawing attention to your products or services. You can showcase new products on Instagram Stories, share reviews from customers, and even run limited-time promotions using this feature. Your audience will be better able to stay informed about your offerings thanks to this, and you will see an increase in traffic to your website or online store.

Sharing user-generated content on Instagram can be done with the help of the Instagram Storytelling feature. User-generated content is a potent tool for increasing both engagement and trust in a brand. You can showcase user-generated content from your followers on Instagram Stories, such as product reviews or customer photos. Your audience will be able to see your brand in action and a sense of community will be fostered as a result.

You can hold competitions or giveaways by using Instagram Storytelling.

On Instagram, holding contests and giving away prizes is an excellent way to build your brand and increase user engagement. You can announce the winners of your contest or giveaway, share user-generated content from the contest, and promote your contest or giveaway all through Instagram Stories. Because of this, your audience will be more likely to remain engaged and enthusiastic about your brand.

Make use of the Instagram Storytelling feature in order to work together with various other brands or influencers.

On Instagram, one of the best ways to build your brand is to work together with other brands or influencers on projects. Make use of Instagram Stories to highlight the results of your collaboration, share user-generated content that was generated as a result of the collaboration, and promote each other's content. You will be able to reach new audiences and build the credibility of your brand with the help of this.

Make use of the Instagram Storytelling feature to distribute instructional material.

The educational content that you create can be easily distributed to your audience using Instagram Stories. You can share helpful hints, tutorials, and guides pertaining to your market or industry by using

Instagram Stories. Your audience will have an easier time seeing you as a thought leader in your industry as a result of this, which will help build trust.

Make use of the Storytelling feature on Instagram to showcase your events.

You can generate a lot of excitement for your upcoming events by showcasing them on Instagram using the Stories feature. You can promote upcoming events, highlight attendees or speakers, and share behind-the-scenes looks at your event all through the use of Instagram Stories. You'll be able to generate buzz and keep your audience up to date thanks to this.

Conclusion

Building your brand on Instagram can be accomplished with the help of an effective tool called "Stories." You can use Instagram Stories to demonstrate the personality of your brand, highlight your products or services, share content generated by users, hold contests or give-aways, collaborate with other brands or influencers, share content that is educational, and demonstrate your events. You can connect with your audience and increase their awareness of your brand by making effective use of the Instagram Storytelling feature. In the following chapter, we will talk about how to engage your followers by using creative captions and hashtags on your Instagram posts.

Chapter 6: Engaging Your Followers with Creative Captions and Hashtags

———

Instagram posts are not complete without a descriptive caption and relevant hashtags. They make it easier for you to connect with your audience, which in turn helps you build engagement and expand your reach. In this chapter, we'll talk about how to engage your followers by coming up with creative captions and hashtags for your Instagram photos.

Make use of captions so that you can tell a story.

When it comes to telling a story and keeping the attention of your audience, captions are a powerful tool. Make use of captions to impart wisdom, pose inquiries, or discuss your perspectives on a subject matter. Make your captions more interesting by incorporating elements of storytelling such as humor, feeling, or suspense into them.

Emojis are a fun way to show personality.

You can give your captions more character and emotion by using emojis, which is a great way to do so. Make use of emojis that are associated with the content you are sharing or that add a personal touch. However, take care not to overuse them as this could cause the meaning of your caption to become muddled.

Increase your audience by using hashtags.

Utilizing hashtags is an excellent strategy for expanding the audience for your posts on Instagram. Make use of hashtags that are pertinent to both the content you are sharing and the audience you are trying to reach. Increase the likelihood of new audiences coming across your content by utilizing a combination of widely used and less common hashtags.

Establish your own branded hashtag.

The creation of a branded hashtag is an excellent way to raise awareness of a brand and encourage users to generate content on their own. Employ a one-of-a-kind hashtag that accurately represents your company, and then motivate your followers to include it in the posts they share. You will be able to increase engagement and the sense of community surrounding your brand if you do this.

Make use of popular hashtags.

Utilizing hashtags that are currently popular is a fantastic way to raise the visibility of your posts and connect with new audiences. Keep an eye on trending hashtags that are relevant to your industry or niche, and be sure to use those hashtags in your posts.

Utilize the suggested hashtags on Instagram.

The content of your post is analyzed by Instagram's hashtag suggestions feature, which then suggests hashtags that are relevant to your post. Make use of this function to learn about new hashtags, which will help you expand the audience for your posts.

Be sure to keep the captions and hashtags current.

Always make sure the captions and hashtags you use are relevant to the content you post and your brand. It's important to steer clear of hashtags and captions that aren't relevant or that give the wrong impression about your brand.

Conclusion

Engaging Instagram posts require a number of essential components, including imaginative captions and hashtags. Use the captions to tell a story, add some personality with emojis, use hashtags to increase reach, create a branded hashtag, use trending hashtags, use Instagram's hashtag suggestions, and make sure that both the captions and the hashtags are still relevant. You can increase engagement and build a stronger connection with your audience by using creative captions and hashtags in an effective manner. In the following chapter, we will go over how to promote your brand through the use of Instagram influencers.

Chapter 7: Building a Loyal Instagram Community through Authenticity and Connection

———

Instagram is not merely a website where users can upload and share photographs and videos. It is a location where you can connect with your target demographic, develop a community, and expand your brand. In this chapter, we'll talk about how to build a loyal community on Instagram by being authentic and connecting with other users.

Be true to yourself.

When it comes to developing a dedicated following on Instagram, authenticity is absolutely essential. Be honest with both your customers and yourself, and steer clear of pretending to be someone you're not. Your audience will value your honesty and authenticity, which will increase the likelihood that they will engage with the content you produce.

Interact with the people watching you.

When it comes to developing a dedicated following on Instagram, active participation from your audience is absolutely necessary. Show your audience that you value their feedback and opinions by responding to their comments, direct messages, and mentions on your content. Building a stronger connection with your audience and developing a sense of community around your brand can be accomplished with the help of the following.

Make use of content generated by users.

The creation of content by users is a powerful tool that can be used to increase engagement and loyalty to a brand. Make use of user-generated content in your posts and Stories to demonstrate your audience's interaction with your brand through their own words. This will assist you in developing a sense of community and will make your audience feel as though they are valuable to you.

Giveaways and competitions should be held on Instagram.

Instagram contests and giveaways are great ways to build engagement with your audience and reward them for their loyalty. Hold giveaways and competitions that are in line with your brand and offer something of value to the people who follow you online. This will assist you in developing a community that is dedicated to your brand.

Engage in joint ventures with competing brands or key opinion leaders.

Working together with other brands or influential people is a fantastic way to expand your brand's exposure to new demographics and strengthen its reputation among existing customers. Collaborate with other brands or influencers who have an audience and set of values similar to your own. Because of this, you will be able to strengthen your connection with your audience and extend the scope of your influence.

Provide value to your audience

It is critical to the success of developing a loyal following on Instagram to provide value to your audience. Develop content for your audience that will either educate, entertain, or inspire them. Make use of your expertise to produce content for your audience that either addresses the challenges they face or offers them fresh perspectives.

The important thing is to stay consistent.

When it comes to cultivating a devoted following on Instagram, consistency is essential. Maintaining your audience's engagement and keeping them up to date requires posting frequently and at regular intervals. Utilize Instagram Analytics to ascertain the optimal posting times for your content and to optimize it for the highest possible level of engagement.

Conclusion

Developing a faithful following on Instagram requires authenticity, engagement, and connection with other users. Maintain your authenticity, interact with your audience, make use of user-generated content, run giveaways and contests on Instagram, collaborate with other brands or influencers, offer your audience something of value, and be consistent. You'll be able to cultivate an active and devoted following on Instagram for your brand if you follow the advice in this article. In the following chapter, we will talk about how to measure and improve the performance of your Instagram account.

Chapter 8: Utilizing Instagram Insights: How to Measure Your Success

---

I nstagram Insights is a powerful tool that offers insightful data regarding your audience, engagement, and the performance of your content. In this chapter, we will go over how to use Instagram Insights to measure your success and improve your Instagram strategy. Insights can be found in the profile section of your Instagram account.

Using Instagram's Analytics and Insights

Go to your Instagram profile and tap the three horizontal lines that are located in the top right corner of the screen. This will take you to your Instagram Insights. To access your data from this location, tap the "Insights" button.

Acquiring Knowledge of Your Audience

The information that Instagram Insights provides about your audience, such as their ages, genders, locations, and interests, is extremely helpful. Make use of these data to improve the quality of your content and produce content that will appeal to your intended audience.

Measuring engagement

When it comes to gauging how successful you are on Instagram, engagement is one of the most important metrics. The Instagram Insights feature makes it possible to view information regarding a post's number of likes, comments, shares, and saves. Make use of this information to determine which posts are doing well and to optimize your content so that it generates the most amount of engagement possible.

Monitoring the expansion of one's following

Monitoring the increase in the number of people who follow you on Instagram is an essential part of gauging your level of success there. Instagram Insights gives you information about the growth of your follower count over time, including both gains and losses. Make use of this data to optimize your content strategy and determine which types of content are leading to an increase in the number of your followers.

Conducting an analysis of reach and impressions

When it comes to measuring the reach of your content, important metrics to track include reach and impressions. The difference between impressions and reach is that impressions measure the total number of times your content has been viewed, whereas reach only accounts for the number of unique users who have seen your content. Make use of this data to improve the quality of your content and expand your audience.

Keeping an eye on the Instagram Stories

Instagram Stories are an effective method for increasing user engagement and developing your online brand using the service. Instagram Insights gives you information about the number of people who viewed, exited, and engaged with your Story. Make use of this data to improve the quality of your Instagram Stories and optimize your Instagram Story strategy.

Increasing the effectiveness of your content strategy

Instagram Insights gives you access to useful information regarding the performance of your content, such as the optimal times to post, the categories of content that do well, and the hashtags that are most likely to generate engagement. Make use of these data to improve your content strategy and produce content that is more interesting to your audience.

Establishing objectives and keeping tabs on progress

It is essential to measure your success on Instagram by setting goals for yourself. Make use of Instagram Insights to establish concrete, measurable objectives, such as boosting engagement or expanding the number of followers. Maintain a consistent monitoring of your progress and adapt your approach to meet your objectives as circumstances change.

Conclusion

It is essential to make use of Instagram Insights in order to accurately gauge your level of success on the platform and make improvements to your content strategy. Utilize Instagram Insights to get a better understanding of your audience, monitor Instagram Stories, optimize your content strategy, analyze reach and impressions, measure engagement, track follower growth, analyze reach and impressions, monitor Instagram Stories, and set goals and track progress. You will be able to gauge your level of success on Instagram and build a more robust and interesting presence there if you make smart use of the Instagram Insights feature.

Chapter 9: The Art of Influencer Marketing on Instagram

———

When it comes to expanding a brand's reach to new audiences and promoting their goods or services on Instagram, influencer marketing has emerged as a popular strategy in recent years. In this chapter, we will talk about the art of influencer marketing on Instagram and how to use the platform to promote your brand in an efficient manner.

Specifying both your objectives and your plan of attack

You need to first determine your objectives and approach before beginning your influencer marketing campaign on Instagram. Determine what it is you hope to accomplish through the use of influencer marketing, such as raising the profile of your brand or increasing sales. Create a strategy that is in line with your objectives and focuses on reaching the appropriate influencers.

Finding out who the influencers are

When it comes to influencer marketing on Instagram, finding the right influencers to work with is absolutely essential. Search for influencers whose audiences and brand values are compatible with those you want to attract. Utilize programs such as HypeAuditor and Followerwonk to perform an analysis of the authenticity, level of engagement, and audience demographics of influencers.

Developing relationships with key opinion leaders and decision-makers

When engaging in influencer marketing on Instagram, it is essential to develop a relationship with the influencers you target. Introduce yourself and your brand to influencers by contacting them through direct messages (DMs) or email. Establish a partnership with the influencer that will be beneficial to both parties by providing them with something of value, such as free products or exclusive access.

Developing original and genuine content

When it comes to influencer marketing on Instagram, authenticity is absolutely essential. Give influencers the opportunity to create content that is consistent with their own personal brand and style while still promoting your company's product or service. Give some guidelines and get some feedback to make sure the content is up to your standards for the brand.

Disclosure of any sponsored material

It is important to disclose sponsored content in order to maintain transparency with your audience and to build their trust. Disclosure of sponsored content is required by law. Make sure that sponsored content is disclosed by influencers by requiring them to use the appropriate hashtags, such as #ad or #sponsored.

Monitoring and improving the outcomes of your efforts

When engaging in influencer marketing on Instagram, it is essential to keep track of your results and work to improve them. Tracking engagement, reach, and new follower growth for influencer marketing campaigns can be done with Instagram Insights. Make use of these data to improve the effectiveness of your influencer marketing strategy and further optimize it.

Keeping relationships with influential people alive and well

When engaging in influencer marketing on Instagram, it is essential to foster and nurture relationships with influencers. Maintain an ongoing working relationship with key influencers by cooperating with them on upcoming campaigns and providing them with value. Construct a web of partnerships with influencers that are intended to last for an extended period of time in order to generate a consistent and powerful brand presence on the platform.

Conclusion

The use of influencer marketing on Instagram can be an effective method for expanding your brand's reach to new audiences and increasing brand awareness. Define your goals and strategy, find influencers, build relationships with influencers, create authentic content, disclose sponsored content, measure and optimize your results, and maintain relationships with influencers. Those are the steps you need to take. You'll be able to make effective use of influencer marketing if you follow these guidelines, which will also help you build a stronger and more engaging presence on Instagram.

Chapter 10: Partnering with Other Brands on Instagram for Maximum Exposure

———

O n Instagram, forming strategic alliances with other brands can be an excellent way to expand your brand's reach and visibility among users of the platform. In this chapter, we'll go over the best ways to collaborate with other brands on Instagram so that you can get the most exposure possible.

Finding the most appropriate brands to collaborate with

Finding the appropriate brands to collaborate with is absolutely necessary if you want to make the most of your exposure on Instagram. Search for brands that share your core beliefs and appeal to the customers you want. Think about forming partnerships with brands that complement your own by providing customers with products or services that are distinct but related.

Creating a relationship that is beneficial to both parties

When collaborating with other brands on Instagram, it's important to work toward creating a relationship that benefits both parties. Determine what each brand has to offer the other and work together to create a partnership that is beneficial to both brands. This could take the form of jointly producing content, organizing events, or providing customers with access to special discounts or sales.

Developing content that is both genuine and interesting

When partnering with other brands on Instagram, it is important to produce content that is both genuine and engaging. Create content together that promotes both of your brands and strikes a chord with the audience you're trying to reach. Make use of Instagram's carousel feature to display the various goods and services offered by both brands.

Leveraging Instagram Stories

When partnering with other brands, making use of Instagram Stories is an excellent way to increase the amount of exposure you receive. Utilize the Instagram Stories feature to provide behind-the-scenes looks at your partnership, promote joint events, or share exclusive content with your audience. You'll be able to engage a greater number of people and reach a wider audience thanks to this.

Tagging and mentioning partner brands

When you want to get the most out of your presence on Instagram, it is essential to tag and mention partner brands in the posts you create. Include the brand names of your partner companies in your posts and encourage those companies to share your content on their own social media profiles. You'll be able to reach more people and raise more people's awareness of your brand with this strategy.

Monitoring and improving the outcomes of your efforts

When partnering with other brands on Instagram, it is important to measure and optimize your results as soon as possible. Make use of Instagram Insights to monitor partnership campaigns' progress regarding engagement, reach, and follower growth. Make use of this information to improve the results of your partnership strategy and optimize it.

Establishing partnerships for the long term

It is essential to cultivate long-term partnerships with other brands on Instagram if you want to make the most of your exposure and build the credibility of your brand. Find other companies whose core beliefs and customer base are compatible with your own, and work out a partnership with them that will be mutually beneficial over the long term. Because of this, you will be able to construct a reliable and powerful presence for your brand on the platform.

Conclusion

Increasing your visibility on Instagram by forming strategic alliances with other brands is one of the most effective strategies you can use. Find the right brands to partner with, develop a relationship that is beneficial to both parties, produce content that is genuine and interesting, make use of Instagram Stories, tag and mention partner brands, measure and improve your results, and establish long-term partnerships. You'll be able to increase the number of people who see your posts on Instagram and build a stronger, more engaging presence on the platform if you follow the advice in this article.

Chapter 11: Instagram Advertising: Strategies for Running Effective Ads

———

A dvertising on Instagram can be an effective method for expanding your reach to new audiences and promoting your brand on the platform. In this section, we'll go over some best practices for efficiently managing Instagram advertisements.

Determine both your objectives and your intended audience.

When it comes to running successful Instagram ads, clearly defining your objectives and intended audience is essential. Establish what it is you hope to accomplish by advertising on Instagram, such as raising consumers' awareness of your brand or increasing sales. Determine who your ideal customers are by looking at their demographics, interests, and activities.

Pick the best format for your advertisement.

When it comes to running successful ads on Instagram, selecting the appropriate ad format is critical. Instagram users can choose from a number of different ad formats, such as photo ads, video ads, carousel ads, and ads within Stories. Pick the type of advertisement that works best for reaching both your goals and the people you want to reach.

Make use of visuals and copy that grab people's attention.

When you want your Instagram ads to be successful, it's important to use visuals and copy that grab people's attention. Make use of visually appealing content that is pertinent to both your brand and your message. Copywriting requires you to be succinct, persuasive, and in tune with the voice of your brand.

Make use of the available targeting options to communicate with the ideal audience.

The targeting options provided by Instagram are a potent instrument for reaching the appropriate audience. Reaching the audience that is most likely to interact with your content can be accomplished through the use of targeting options that are based on demographics, interests, behaviors, and location.

Make use of call-to-actions, also known as CTAs, in order to drive conversions.

It is essential to make use of CTAs in order to drive conversions through Instagram ads. Make sure the calls to action you use are easy to understand, compelling, and in line with your overall goals. Utilize the call-to-action (CTA) buttons that Instagram provides, such as "Learn More" and "Shop Now," to make it simple for users to take the desired course of action.

Keep an eye on, and improve, your advertisements.

When it comes to running effective Instagram ads, monitoring and optimizing your advertisements is essential. Utilize Instagram's Ads Manager to keep track of how well your advertisements are performing in terms of engagement, reach, and conversions. Make use of these data to improve the effectiveness of your advertisements and increase your profits.

Experiment with a variety of different ads.

When it comes to running successful Instagram ads, testing out different ad variations is an essential step. To determine which variations of visuals, copy, targeting options, and ad formats produce the best results, test a variety of different combinations. Make use of these data to improve the effectiveness of your advertisements and increase your profits.

Conclusion

Advertising on Instagram can be a powerful tool for expanding your reach to new audiences and promoting your brand within the Instagram ecosystem. Define your goals and your intended audience, select the appropriate ad format, make use of captivating visuals and copy, make use of targeting options to reach the intended audience, make use of call-to-actions to drive conversions, monitor and optimize your ads, and test out different variations of your ads. You'll be able to successfully run ads on Instagram and achieve the advertising goals you set for the platform if you follow the advice in this article.

Chapter 12: How to Use Instagram Live for Business Success

Businesses have a powerful resource at their disposal with Instagram Live to connect with their audience in real time and promote their brand on the platform they use. In this chapter, we'll go over the best ways to utilize Instagram Live for your company's benefit.

Make a plan for both the content and the promotion.

When using Instagram Live for your business, it is critical to carefully plan both the content you will share and the promotion strategy you will employ. Determine the subject matter or overarching themes that you want to cover in your live videos, and then promote those videos on your Instagram profile and other social media channels.

Interact in real time with the people who are watching you.

The primary advantage of using Instagram Live is the ability to interact with your audience in real time. During the course of your live video, you should actively encourage viewers to submit questions or comments and then respond to these in real time. Building a stronger connection with your audience and developing a sense of community around your brand can be accomplished with the help of the following.

Launch new products and make important announcements with Instagram Live.

Utilizing Instagram Live to make product announcements and launches is a fantastic way to generate excitement and buzz about your company and its products. Utilize Instagram Live to introduce brand-new products or services while simultaneously showcasing their various features and the advantages they provide in real-time.

Engage in joint ventures with competing brands or key opinion leaders.

On Instagram Live, establishing credibility for your brand and reaching new audiences can be accomplished to a great extent by partnering with other brands or influencers. Collaborate with other brands or influencers who have an audience and set of values similar to your own. You will be able to reach a larger audience this way, in addition to strengthening the connection you have with the audience you already have.

Conduct question-and-answer sessions and interviews.

Engaging with your audience and providing value to them can be accomplished through the use of Instagram Live by conducting question-and-answer sessions and interviews. You can respond to questions or conduct interviews with industry leaders by using Instagram Live. This will assist you in establishing yourself as an authority within your field and in building trust with the audience you are addressing.

Promote your Instagram Live videos

It is important to promote your Instagram Live videos if you want to maximize the reach and engagement of those videos. You can promote your live videos to your audience and encourage them to tune in by posting about them on Instagram Stories as well as other social media channels. Make use of the appropriate hashtags in order to attract a larger audience and promote your live videos to the subscribers on your email list.

Repurpose the videos you've recorded on Instagram Live.

The best way to make the most of the value and reach of your Instagram Live videos is to reuse and repurpose them. Keep a copy of your live videos so that you can convert them into other forms of content in the future, such as blog posts, podcasts, or videos on YouTube. You will be able to reach a larger audience this way, in addition to providing value to the audience you already have.

Conclusion

Businesses have a powerful resource at their disposal with Instagram Live to connect with their audience in real time and promote their brand on the platform they use. You should plan your content and promotion strategy, engage with your audience in real time, use Instagram Live for product launches and announcements, collaborate with other brands or influencers, host question-and-answer sessions and interviews, promote your Instagram Live videos, and repurpose your Instagram Live videos. You'll be able to get the most out of Instagram Live if you follow these guidelines, which will also help you establish a stronger and more engaging presence on the platform.

Chapter 13: Instagram IGTV: A Guide to Creating Engaging Video Content

―――

For companies looking to create long-form video content and connect with new audiences on Instagram, IGTV is a powerful tool that they can leverage. A step-by-step tutorial on how to produce interesting video content for Instagram's IGTV platform is going to be covered in this chapter.

Prepare a content strategy for your website.

It is critical to plan out your content strategy before beginning work on the production of engaging video content for Instagram IGTV. Find out what kinds of subjects or themes you want to cover in your videos, and think about how those things relate to your audience and brand. Create a content calendar to guarantee that your posting schedule will remain unchanged.

Develop video content that is both high-quality and interesting.

It is essential to produce video content that is both high in quality and interesting if you want to attract and keep an audience on Instagram IGTV. To produce videos that will resonate with your audience, it is important to use audio and visuals of a high quality and to tell engaging stories. Make your videos accessible to a greater number of people by including captions or subtitles in them.

Ensure that your video's title and description are optimized.

It is important to optimize both the title and description of your video in order to increase the likelihood that it will be discovered on IGTV. Make sure the titles of your videos are understandable and detailed, and that they accurately reflect the contents of the videos. You can improve your search rankings by using descriptions to provide more context and including relevant keywords in those descriptions.

Increase your discoverability by making use of hashtags and tags.

Increasing the discoverability of your Instagram IGTV videos requires the use of hashtags and tags, both of which are important. It is important to make use of hashtags that are both relevant and targeted if you want users to be able to find your videos through search or explore. You can increase your reach and engagement by tagging other relevant accounts, such as those belonging to brands or influencers.

Promote your IGTV videos

It is essential to promote your IGTV videos if you want to maximize the reach and engagement of your content. You can promote your IGTV videos and encourage your audience to watch them by posting about them on Instagram, using Instagram Stories, and using other social media channels. Make use of the appropriate hashtags and tags in order to attract a larger audience.

Track your progress and strive to improve.

When it comes to producing engaging video content for Instagram IGTV, measuring and optimizing your results are two steps that are essential. You can monitor the growth of engagement, views, and followers for your IGTV videos through the Instagram Insights app. Make use of these data to improve your content strategy and overall results by optimizing them.

Engage in joint ventures with competing brands or key opinion leaders.

On Instagram's IGTV platform, collaborating with other brands or influencers is an excellent way to reach new audiences and to build credibility for one's own brand. Collaborate with other brands or influencers who have an audience and set of values similar to your own. You will be able to reach a larger audience this way, in addition to strengthening the connection you have with the audience you already have.

Conclusion

For companies looking to create long-form video content and connect with new audiences on Instagram, IGTV is a powerful tool that they can leverage. Plan your content strategy, produce high-quality and engaging video content, optimize the title and description of your video, make use of hashtags and tags to increase discoverability, promote your IGTV videos, measure and optimize your results, and work together with other brands or influencers. You'll be able to build a stronger and more engaging presence on the platform by following these guidelines, which will allow you to create engaging video content for Instagram IGTV.

Chapter 14: Creating a Winning Instagram Content Strategy

———

B uilding a powerful and engaging presence on Instagram requires having a winning content strategy to implement on the platform. In this chapter, we are going to talk about how to create a content strategy that is successful on Instagram.

Determine the core values and messaging of your brand.

When developing a winning content strategy for Instagram, it is essential to first define the values and messaging of your brand. Find out what your company stands for and what you want the audience to take away from your message by determining these things. You will be able to create content that is meaningful to your audience and builds the credibility of your brand with the help of this.

Identify your target audience

Establishing who your ideal followers are on Instagram is a crucial step in developing a winning content strategy for the platform. Find out who your audience is by looking at their demographics, their interests, and their behaviors. Make use of this information to create content that is pertinent to your audience as well as engaging for them.

Develop a content calendar

Building a consistent and interesting Instagram presence requires the creation of a content calendar, which is an important step in the process. Prepare your content in advance, and devise a publishing schedule that takes into account both your long-term objectives and the people you intend to reach. You can maintain the freshness and interest of your content by utilizing a variety of content formats, such as photos, videos, Stories, and IGTV.

Utilize a variety of topics for the content.

It is important to use a variety of content themes in order to maintain the variety and engagement of your Instagram content. Utilize topics that are congruent with the core values and messaging of your brand, such as exclusive behind-the-scenes looks, user-generated content, product spotlights, or industry news. You will find that doing so will assist you in developing a rounded Instagram presence that is appealing to your audience.

Make use of captivating visuals as well as copy.

When developing a winning content strategy for Instagram, it is essential to make use of captivating visuals and copy. Make use of visuals of a high quality that showcase both your brand and your message. Copywriting requires you to be succinct, persuasive, and in tune with the voice of your brand. Make your content more engaging by including captions, emojis, and hashtags in your posts.

Make use of Instagram's various features.

When developing a successful content strategy for Instagram, it is critical to make effective use of the platform's features. Make use of Instagram features such as Stories, IGTV, and Reels to develop content that is interesting and varied. You can foster a sense of community around your brand by using Instagram Live to connect with your audience in real time and share content.

Track your progress and strive to improve.

When it comes to developing a winning content strategy for Instagram, it is essential to measure and improve upon your results. Utilize

Instagram Insights to monitor the level of engagement, reach, and growth in the number of followers your content receives. Make use of these data to improve your content strategy and overall results by optimizing them.

Conclusion

Building a powerful and engaging presence on Instagram requires having a winning content strategy to implement on the platform. Define the values and messaging of your brand, determine who your target audience is, create a content calendar, use a variety of content themes, employ engaging visuals and copy, make use of Instagram's features, measure and optimize your results, and so on. If you follow these guidelines, you will be able to develop a successful content strategy for Instagram that will resonate with your audience and build the credibility of your brand on the platform.

Chapter 15: Tips for Creating Instagram Content that Converts

———

Creating content for Instagram that is engaging and ultimately leads to a purchase is essential to increasing sales and achieving business success on the platform. In this chapter, we'll go over some best practices for developing content for Instagram that generates conversions.

Make use of call-to-actions (CTAs) that are unmistakable and convincing.

When it comes to increasing conversions on Instagram, one of the most important things to do is to use CTAs that are both clear and convincing. Use calls to action (CTAs) that are in line with your goals and the audience you are trying to reach, such as "Shop Now" or "Learn More." Make it easy for users to take action by utilizing Instagram's Calls to Action buttons.

Put on display any products or services you offer.

When it comes to increasing sales on Instagram, one of the most important things you can do is showcase your products or services. To effectively demonstrate the features and advantages of the goods or services you offer, you should make use of images of high quality and persuasive writing. Make it simple for users to buy your products by utilizing the product tags and shopping features that are available on Instagram.

Utilize user-generated content, also known as UGC.

Utilizing user-generated content (UGC) is critical to gaining the trust and credibility of your audience on Instagram. You should encourage your followers to share content on Instagram that features your products or services and that they have created. Make use of this user-generated content in your own content in order to demonstrate real-world applications of your products or services.

Leverage relationships with influential people.

Establishing a credible presence on Instagram and connecting with new users is made much easier when partnerships with influential users are utilized. Create a partnership with influential people who have the same audience and values as you. Make use of their content to drive sales of your products or services by promoting your own content.

Use social proof

When it comes to establishing trust and credibility with your audience on Instagram, using social proof is an important step. Make use of customer reviews, ratings, and testimonials to demonstrate the value and quality of the goods or services you provide. Make a specific area for displaying social proof by utilizing the highlights feature of Instagram Stories or IGTV.

Make use of deals or promotions that have a time limit.

Creating a sense of urgency and driving sales on Instagram can be accomplished very effectively through the use of time-sensitive offers or promotions. As an incentive for users to purchase your goods or services, you can run promotions such as flash sales, which offer deep discounts or even free shipping. You can promote your time-sensitive offers by using the Stories or posts features on Instagram.

Employ the services of Instagram's paid advertising.

When it comes to increasing conversions on Instagram, making use of Instagram's paid advertising is critical. Make use of Instagram's Ads Manager in order to create targeted advertisements that deliver the appropriate message to the appropriate audience. Make use of Instagram's conversion tracking feature to evaluate the efficacy of your advertisements and improve your overall performance.

Conclusion

Creating content for Instagram that is engaging and ultimately leads to a purchase is essential to increasing sales and achieving business success on the platform. Utilize call-to-actions that are crystal clear and persuasive, highlight your products or services, utilize user-generated content, utilize influencer partnerships, utilize social proof, utilize limited-time offers or promotions, and utilize Instagram's paid advertising. You will be able to generate content for Instagram that will drive conversions and help you achieve your business goals on the platform if you follow the advice in this article.

Chapter 16: Monetizing Your Instagram Account: How to Make Money on the Platform

———

Your presence on Instagram can be turned into a source of income by taking advantage of the myriad opportunities provided by Instagram to monetize your account. How to make money on Instagram is the topic that will be covered in this chapter.

Posts that are sponsored as well as collaborations

When it comes to monetizing your Instagram account, sponsored posts and collaborations are two of the most popular options. If you create content highlighting a brand's products or services, or if you promote that brand on your account, the brand may pay you for your work. You can work with influencer marketing agencies that connect influencers and brands in order to find sponsorship opportunities, or you can reach out directly to brands whose ideals and customer base are compatible with your own.

Internet marketing via affiliates

When you promote the goods or services of other companies through your Instagram account using affiliate marketing, you open up the possibility of earning commissions. You can share your one-of-a-kind affiliate link in your posts or Stories by becoming a member of the affiliate programs of companies whose products and services are compatible with both your core beliefs and the people you intend to reach. You will receive a commission for any purchases made by your followers that are made using your affiliate link.

Promote and sell various goods and services

If you own a company or an online store, selling items or services through your Instagram account is a fantastic way to generate revenue from the platform. You can make it simple for your followers to buy your products by utilizing Instagram's shopping features or by including product tags in your posts. Your Instagram account can also be used to advertise your services, such as consulting or coaching, to potential clients.

Produce and market your own digital goods.

Creating and selling digital products on Instagram, such as e-books, courses, or templates, is an additional way to generate revenue from your account on that platform. You are able to make it simple for your followers to buy the digital products you promote on your account by utilizing Instagram's shopping features or product tags. This will allow you to increase sales.

Make your followers aware of sponsored content that they can access.

If you have a large and active following on Instagram, one of the best ways to make money off of your account is to make sponsored content available to your followers. You can create sponsored content on your followers' behalf, or you can offer to promote the content or businesses of your followers in exchange for payment. This could be a way to support your followers while also monetizing your account, so it would be beneficial to everyone involved.

Sell access to exclusive content

Selling access to exclusive content on your Instagram account, such as behind-the-scenes looks or additional advice and guidance, is an excellent way to generate revenue from your account. It is possible for you to establish a membership program or a subscription service in which your followers pay a fee in exchange for access to special content.

Employ the services of Instagram's paid advertising.

If you run a company or sell goods or services, one of the best ways to make money off of your Instagram account is to make use of the paid advertising features that Instagram provides. Utilizing Instagram's Ads Manager, you are able to produce targeted advertisements that convey the intended message to the intended audience. Make use of Instagram's conversion tracking feature to evaluate the efficacy of your advertisements and improve your overall performance.

Conclusion

Your presence on Instagram can become a source of income by monetizing your account, which is a great way to make the most of the platform. Your Instagram account can be monetized in a variety of ways, including through sponsored posts and collaborations, affiliate marketing, the sale of physical or digital products, the promotion of paid access to exclusive content, the creation and sale of digital products, the provision of sponsored content to your followers, and the use of paid advertising on Instagram. You'll be able to monetize your Instagram account and accomplish your business goals on the platform if you follow the advice in this article.

Chapter 17: Building a Winning Instagram E-Commerce Strategy

───

Instagram is a powerful e-commerce platform, with features that enable businesses to sell products directly to consumers on the platform. This allows businesses to bypass the middleman and bypass traditional retail channels. In this chapter, we will go over the best practices for developing a successful e-commerce strategy for Instagram.

Use Instagram Shopping

Utilization of Instagram Shopping is critical to the development of a successful e-commerce strategy for Instagram. Instagram Shopping enables businesses to tag products in their posts or Stories and add a "Shop Now" button that links directly to the product page on their website. This feature is only available to businesses with a verified Instagram account. In order for businesses to make use of Instagram Shopping, they will first need to create a product catalog on Facebook.

Produce images of the product that are of a high quality.

When it comes to increasing sales on Instagram, having high-quality visuals of your products is essential. Utilize product images or videos of a high clarity and production quality that highlight the features and advantages of the products you sell. Make use of compelling copy that draws attention to the benefits of your products and helps them stand out from the competition in a crowded feed.

Utilize Instagram Highlights as well as Stories.

When developing a comprehensive strategy for e-commerce on Instagram, it is critical to make use of Instagram Stories and Instagram Highlights. Make use of Instagram Stories to advertise your wares, provide customers with access to special sales or discounts, and give an inside look at the workings of your company. You can showcase your products or categories on Instagram by using the Highlights feature, or you can create dedicated highlights for promotions or sales.

Use Instagram Ads

It is essential to make use of Instagram Ads if one wishes to reach new audiences and increase sales on the platform. Make use of Instagram's Ads Manager in order to create targeted advertisements that deliver the appropriate message to the appropriate audience. Make use of Instagram's conversion tracking feature to evaluate the efficacy of your advertisements and improve your overall performance.

Collaborate with those who have influence.

Working together with Instagram users who already have a significant following can be an excellent way to expand your reach and establish credibility on the platform. Create a partnership with influential people who have the same audience and values as you. Make use of their content to drive sales of your products and promote your brand.

Use Instagram Live

When it comes to building a sense of community around your brand and driving sales on the platform, utilizing Instagram Live is critical. Make use of Instagram Live to provide real-time demonstrations of your wares, announce limited-time sales or discounts, or respond to inquiries posed by your target audience.

Track your progress and strive to improve.

When developing a winning strategy for Instagram e-commerce, it is essential to measure your results and make adjustments based on those measurements. Utilize Instagram Insights to monitor the level of engagement, reach, and sales generated by your online store's content. Make use of these data to improve your content strategy and overall results by optimizing them.

Conclusion

The development of a successful e-commerce strategy for Instagram is absolutely necessary for increasing sales and achieving commercial success on the platform. Utilize Instagram Shopping, produce high-quality visuals of your products, utilize Instagram Stories and Instagram Highlights, utilize Instagram Ads, work with influencers, utilize Instagram Live, measure and optimize your results, and utilize Instagram Live. You'll be able to develop a successful Instagram e-commerce strategy and accomplish your business goals on the platform if you follow the advice in this article.

Chapter 18: Leveraging Instagram Shopping: A Guide for Online Retailers

---

Instagram Shopping is a useful application for online retailers because it enables companies to sell their wares to end users directly from within the Instagram app itself. In this chapter, we will go over how to make the most of Instagram Shopping to increase sales for your online retail company.

Establish your online product catalog.

The first step in maximizing your potential with Instagram Shopping is to organize your product catalog. This can be accomplished by connecting your Instagram account to your Facebook page and creating a product catalog using the Facebook Business Manager app. Check to see that the information and prices listed in your product catalog are correct and up to date at all times.

Make posts that can be purchased.

In order to drive sales on Instagram, it is important to create posts that can be shopped. When showcasing your products, make sure to use product visuals of a high quality and copy that is interesting. Tag your products whenever you share a post or a Story, and include a "Shop Now" button that takes readers directly to the page on your website where they can purchase the item.

Utilize the shopping features provided by Instagram.

It is essential to make use of Instagram Shopping's shopping features in order to maximize its potential. Make it simple for your followers to buy the products you sell on the platform by taking advantage of functionalities such as product tags, shopping from creators, and shopping from reels.

Utilize Instagram Highlights as well as Stories.

When developing a comprehensive strategy for Instagram Shopping, it is critical to make use of Instagram Stories and Instagram Highlights. Make use of Instagram Stories to advertise your wares, provide customers with access to special sales or discounts, and give an inside look at the workings of your company. You can showcase your products or categories on Instagram by using the Highlights feature, or you can create dedicated highlights for promotions or sales.

Use Instagram Ads

It is essential to make use of Instagram Ads if one wishes to reach new audiences and increase sales on the platform. Make use of Instagram's Ads Manager in order to create targeted advertisements that deliver the appropriate message to the appropriate audience. Make use of Instagram's conversion tracking feature to evaluate the efficacy of your advertisements and improve your overall performance.

Collaborate with those who have influence.

Working together with Instagram users who already have a significant following can be an excellent way to expand your reach and establish credibility on the platform. Create a partnership with influential people who have the same audience and values as you. Make use of their content to drive sales of your products and promote your brand.

Track your progress and strive to improve.

When maximizing the potential of Instagram Shopping, it is essential to conduct thorough analysis of your results and make adjustments as necessary. Utilize Instagram Insights to monitor the level of engagement, reach, and sales generated by your online store's content. Make use of these data to improve your content strategy and overall results by optimizing them.

Conclusion

Utilizing Instagram Shopping to its full potential is essential for online retailers on the platform who wish to increase sales and achieve commercial success. Establish your product catalog, make your posts shoppable, make use of Instagram's shopping features, use Instagram Stories and Instagram Highlights, make use of Instagram Ads, work with influencers, measure and improve your results, and collaborate with them. You can use Instagram Shopping to drive sales for your online retail business that's hosted on the platform by following these tips and putting them into action.

Chapter 19: Building Your Personal Brand on Instagram: Tips for Entrepreneurs

———

Creating a personal brand on Instagram is an important way for business owners to promote their companies, establish themselves as thought leaders in their industries, and build a following of devoted customers and fans. In the following section, we will go over some suggestions for developing your personal brand on Instagram.

Define the identity of your brand.

When it comes to developing a powerful personal brand on Instagram, defining the identity of your brand is an essential step. Find out what sets you apart from others in your field and think about what you'd like to be known for in general. Make use of this information to develop a consistent brand identity that will be reflected in the content, visuals, and messaging that you produce.

Make use of images of a high quality.

When it comes to developing a powerful personal brand on Instagram, the use of visuals of a high-quality is critical. Make use of high-resolution images and videos that highlight your individuality, sense of style, and the identity of your brand. Create a unified visual identity by utilizing elements of branding such as color, font, and design that are consistent with one another.

Make sure the content is interesting.

The development of an interesting personal brand on Instagram relies heavily on the production of interesting content. Make use of a variety of content types, such as photos, videos, and Stories, to illustrate who you are as a person, as well the areas in which you excel, and the things that interest you. Make use of copy that is interesting, reflects the voice of your brand, and encourages conversation between you and your audience.

Interact with the people who are watching.

When it comes to developing a powerful personal brand on Instagram, one of the most important things you can do is engage with your audience. Ask your followers questions, respond to their comments and direct messages, and encourage them to engage in conversation with you. Make use of the polls, questions, and quizzes that are available on Instagram to engage with your audience and gain a deeper understanding of them.

Cooperate with the other people.

On Instagram, building your personal brand through collaboration with other users is an effective strategy. Create content together with other business owners or thought leaders in your field; host events; or offer promotions and discounts jointly with these individuals. You may be able to reach new audiences and establish yourself as a thought leader in your industry with the assistance of this.

Use Instagram Live

Utilizing Instagram Live is essential in order to construct a solid foundation for one's personal brand on Instagram. You can demonstrate your level of expertise, hold question-and-answer sessions, or provide an insider's look at your company by using Instagram Live. This can assist you in connecting with your audience and gaining their trust while also enhancing your credibility in their eyes.

Utilize Instagram Highlights as well as Stories.

When it comes to developing a powerful personal brand on Instagram, making effective use of Instagram Stories and Highlights is essential. You can keep your followers updated on your day-to-day life, highlight your interests, or provide them with access to exclusive content by using Instagram Stories. You can create a portfolio of your work, share your beliefs and values, or highlight your expertise by using Instagram's Highlights feature.

Conclusion

For business owners who want to promote their companies, cultivating a loyal following, and establishing themselves as thought leaders, creating a personal brand on Instagram is essential. Define the identity of your brand, utilize visuals of a high quality, produce content that is engaging, interact with your audience, collaborate with others, use Instagram Live, and make use of Instagram Stories and Instagram Highlights. You'll be able to establish a powerful personal brand on Instagram and achieve your business goals on the platform if you follow the advice in this article.

Chapter 20: Instagram for Service-Based Businesses: A Guide for Professionals

———

Instagram is a powerful platform that can help service-based businesses showcase their expertise, establish credibility, and bring in new customers. In this chapter, we will cover a guide for professionals on how to use Instagram for businesses that provide a service to their customers.

Define your target audience

Establishing who your ideal customers are on Instagram is essential to developing a winning strategy for service-based businesses using the platform. Find out who your ideal customers are and what their requirements and problems are by doing some research. Make use of this information to develop content that caters to their requirements and addresses the concerns that they have.

Make use of images of a high quality.

When it comes to developing a credible and professional Instagram presence for service-based businesses, the utilization of visuals of a high-quality is essential. Make use of images and videos with a high resolution to demonstrate your level of expertise and professionalism. Create a unified visual identity by utilizing elements of branding such as color, font, and design that are consistent with one another.

Create educational content

Developing informative content is essential if you want to demonstrate your level of expertise and bring in new customers through Instagram. Make use of a variety of content types, such as photos, videos, and

Stories, to convey your expertise to your audience and provide them with insightful advice and recommendations. Make use of copy that is interesting, reflects the voice of your brand, and encourages conversation between you and your audience.

Interact with the people who are watching.

When it comes to developing new relationships and luring in new customers on Instagram, one of the most important things you can do is engage with your audience. Ask your followers questions, respond to their comments and direct messages, and encourage them to engage in conversation with you. Make use of the polls, questions, and quizzes that are available on Instagram to engage with your audience and gain a deeper understanding of them.

Engage in cooperative efforts with other experts in the field.

The best way to demonstrate your level of expertise and connect with new users on Instagram is to work with other professionals in a collaborative effort. Create content together with other experts in your field, organize events together, and run joint marketing campaigns. Developing your credibility and establishing yourself as a thought leader in your industry can be facilitated by doing so.

Use Instagram Live

Utilizing Instagram Live is essential if you want to demonstrate your expertise and develop meaningful connections with the people who follow you on Instagram. You can use Instagram Live to host question-and-answer sessions, offer advice and suggestions, or provide a look behind the scenes at your company. This can assist you in connecting with your audience and gaining their trust while also enhancing your credibility in their eyes.

Utilize Instagram Highlights as well as Stories.

When attempting to demonstrate your level of expertise and provide insightful guidance to your audience on Instagram, it is critical to make use of the Instagram Stories and Highlights features. You can keep your followers updated on your day-to-day life, highlight your interests, or provide them with access to exclusive content by using Instagram Stories. You can create a portfolio of your work, share your beliefs and values, or highlight your expertise by using Instagram's Highlights feature.

Conclusion

It is essential for businesses that provide services to make use of Instagram to demonstrate their level of expertise, develop their credibility, and bring in new customers. Engage with your audience, create educational content, collaborate with other professionals, use Instagram Live, and utilize Instagram Stories and Instagram Highlights. Defining your target audience, using high-quality visuals, creating educational content, engaging with your audience, and using Instagram Live are all important steps. You'll be able to use Instagram to accomplish your business objectives and expand your service-based business on the platform if you follow the advice in this article.

Chapter 21: Instagram for Brick-and-Mortar Businesses: A Guide for Local Merchants

———

B rick-and-mortar businesses can connect with their local customers, promote their products and services, and drive foot traffic to their physical locations by using Instagram as a powerful platform. In this chapter, we will go over a guide for local merchants on how to use Instagram for their traditional businesses, such as stores and restaurants.

Define your target audience

Establishing who your ideal Instagram followers are is essential to developing a winning strategy for brick-and-mortar businesses using the platform. Find out who your ideal local customers are and what their interests and requirements are, then cater your business to them. Make use of this information to develop content for your products or services that speaks to the interests of your audience and promotes those interests.

Make use of images of a high quality.

In order to create a presence on Instagram that is both professional and appealing for brick-and-mortar businesses, it is essential to use visuals of a high quality. Make use of images and videos with a high resolution that promote both your products or services as well as the location of your business. Create a unified visual identity by utilizing elements of branding such as color, font, and design that are consistent with one another.

Put on display any products or services you offer.

When promoting your traditional offline business on Instagram, it is essential to highlight your offerings, whether they be products or services. Make use of a variety of content types, such as photos, videos, and Stories, to demonstrate the quality of your goods or services and to advertise your physical location. Make use of compelling copy that accurately reflects the voice of your brand and encourages customers to visit your actual location.

Participate actively in the life of your neighborhood.

Building relationships and using Instagram to promote your brick-and-mortar business are both helped along by active participation in the community in which you do business. Ask your followers questions, respond to their comments and direct messages, and encourage them to engage in conversation with you. Make use of features on Instagram such as location tags and local hashtags to connect with local customers and expand your business's reach in the community.

Advertise upcoming events and ongoing promotions

It is important to promote events and sales if you want to increase foot traffic to your physical location and sales for your brick-and-mortar business. Make use of Instagram to spread the word about upcoming events, sales, or other exclusive deals. You can create content specifically geared toward promotions and events by using Instagram Stories and Highlights.

Use Instagram Ads

When it comes to attracting new local customers and increasing foot traffic to your brick-and-mortar store, utilizing Instagram Ads is one of the most important things you can do on the platform. Make use of Instagram's Ads Manager in order to create targeted advertisements that deliver the appropriate message to the appropriate audience. Make use of Instagram's conversion tracking feature to evaluate the efficacy of your advertisements and improve your overall performance.

Use Instagram Live

Utilizing Instagram Live is critical for highlighting the physical location of your business and fostering relationships with the Instagram community in your area. You can use Instagram Live to give your audience a behind-the-scenes look at your company, demonstrate your wares or services, or host question-and-answer sessions with them.

Conclusion

It is essential for brick-and-mortar businesses to use Instagram in order to connect with local customers, promote their products and services, and drive foot traffic to their physical location. These three goals can all be accomplished through Instagram. Define your target audience, make use of high-quality visuals, demonstrate your goods or services, interact with the community around you, promote your events and deals, use Instagram Ads, and make use of Instagram Live. You can use Instagram to accomplish your business goals and grow your offline, brick-and-mortar business on the platform if you follow these tips and procedures.

Chapter 22: Instagram for Non-Profits: A Guide to Raising Awareness and Funds

Instagram is a powerful platform that non-profit organizations can use to raise awareness for their cause, engage with supporters of their mission, and raise funds for their organization. In this chapter, we will go over a guide for non-profit organizations on how they can make the most of Instagram to accomplish their objectives.

Define your mission and values

The first step in developing a successful Instagram strategy for a non-profit organization is to define the organization's mission and values. Find out what sets your company apart from others and what you hope to accomplish with the help of your efforts. Make use of this information to generate content that accurately represents your goals and principles.

Make use of images of a high quality.

It is important for non-profit organizations to use visuals of a high quality in order to create a professional and engaging presence on Instagram. Make use of high-resolution photos and videos that highlight your work and the difference you're making in the world. Create a unified visual identity by utilizing elements of branding such as color, font, and design that are consistent with one another.

Create educational content

It is important to create content that is educational in nature in order to increase awareness and engage with supporters on Instagram. Sharing information about your cause, the work you're doing, and the impact you're making can be accomplished through the use of a variety of content types, including photos, videos, and Stories. Make use of copy that is interesting, reflects the voice of your brand, and encourages conversation between you and your audience.

Interact with the people who are watching.

When it comes to developing relationships and garnering support for your non-profit organization on Instagram, one of the most important things you can do is engage with your audience. Ask your followers questions, respond to their comments and direct messages, and encourage them to engage in conversation with you. Make use of the polls, questions, and quizzes that are available on Instagram to engage with your audience and gain a deeper understanding of them.

Use Instagram Live

When it comes to connecting with your audience and showcasing your work on Instagram in real time, using Instagram Live is an essential tool. You can share updates on your work, give a behind-the-scenes look at your organization, or host Q&A sessions and question and answer sessions through Instagram Live. This can assist you in connecting with your audience and gaining their trust while also enhancing your credibility in their eyes.

Organize and publicize fundraising efforts.

When trying to raise money for your non-profit organization on Instagram, it is essential to promote fundraising campaigns. Make use of Instagram to spread awareness about fundraising campaigns, share stories of their impact, and encourage people to make donations. Create content that is specifically geared toward fundraising efforts by using Instagram Stories and Highlights, and make it simple for supporters to contribute to the cause.

Work together with other charitable organizations and influential people.

On Instagram, a great way to expand your reach to new audiences and garner support for your cause is to work together with other charitable organizations and social influencers. Join forces with other charitable organizations or influential people whose mission and audience align with your own. Make use of their content to spread awareness about your cause and garner support.

Conclusion

It is essential for charities and other non-profit organizations to utilize Instagram in order to increase awareness, engage with supporters, and raise funds for their causes. Define your organization's mission and core values, make use of high-quality visuals, produce educational content, interact with your audience, make use of Instagram Live, promote fundraising campaigns, and work together with other charitable organizations and influential people. You can use Instagram to accomplish the goals of your non-profit organization and make a positive impact in your community if you follow these tips and instructions.

Chapter 23: Instagram for B2B: How to Reach Other Businesses on the Platform

―――――

Instagram is a powerful platform that allows businesses that sell to other businesses to connect with other businesses, showcase their products and services, and build relationships with potential customers. In this chapter, we will go over some helpful hints on how to use Instagram to connect with other businesses that are using the platform.

Define your target audience

Establishing who your ideal followers are on Instagram is one of the most important steps in developing a winning strategy for B2B companies. Find out who your ideal customers are and what their requirements and problems are by doing some research. Make use of this information to develop content that caters to their requirements and addresses the concerns that they have.

Make use of images of a high quality.

When it comes to developing a credible and appealing Instagram presence for B2B companies, the utilization of visuals of a high-quality is an essential component. Make use of images and videos with a high resolution to promote your company's brand identity and show off your products or services. Create a unified visual identity by utilizing elements of branding such as color, font, and design that are consistent with one another.

Create educational content

It is important to create educational content if you want to build credibility with potential customers on Instagram and show them that you are an expert in your field. Make use of a variety of content types, such as photos, videos, and Stories, to convey your expertise to your audience and provide them with insightful advice and recommendations. Make use of copy that is interesting, reflects the voice of your brand, and encourages conversation between you and your audience.

Use relevant hashtags

It is essential to make use of relevant hashtags in order to connect with other businesses and potential customers on Instagram. Make use of hashtags that are specific to your industry and are pertinent to both your company and the audience you are trying to reach. You may be able to connect with potential customers and reach new audiences as a result of this.

Interact with the people who are watching.

Building relationships with potential customers and attracting new followers on Instagram both require active participation from your audience. Ask your followers questions, respond to their comments and direct messages, and encourage them to engage in conversation with you. Make use of the polls, questions, and quizzes that are available on Instagram to engage with your audience and gain a deeper understanding of them.

Utilize Instagram Highlights as well as Stories.

When attempting to showcase your expertise and provide prospective customers on Instagram with helpful insights, it is essential to make use of the Instagram Stories and Highlights features. You can keep your followers updated on your day-to-day life, highlight your interests, or provide them with access to exclusive content by using Instagram

Stories. You can create a portfolio of your work, share your beliefs and values, or highlight your expertise by using Instagram's Highlights feature.

Use Instagram Ads

When trying to reach new businesses and potential customers on Instagram, it is important to make use of Instagram's advertising features. Make use of Instagram's Ads Manager in order to create targeted advertisements that deliver the appropriate message to the appropriate audience. Make use of Instagram's conversion tracking feature to evaluate the efficacy of your advertisements and improve your overall performance.

Conclusion

Utilizing Instagram for business-to-business (B2B) purposes is essential for reaching out to other companies, demonstrating your level of expertise, and forming connections with prospective customers. Engage with your audience, create educational content, use relevant hashtags, use Instagram Stories and Highlights, and make use of Instagram Ads. Defining your target audience, using high-quality visuals, creating educational content, using relevant hashtags, and using Instagram Ads are all important steps. If you follow these guidelines, you will be able to use Instagram to accomplish your B2B business goals and connect with new customers on the platform.

Chapter 24: The Power of Instagram Influencers in B2B Marketing

---

Instagram influencers are not limited to being used by B2C companies only. Collaborating with influential people can also be beneficial for business-to-business (B2B) companies in terms of reaching their target audience, raising brand awareness, and establishing credibility in their field. The power of Instagram influencers in business-to-business marketing will be the topic of discussion in this chapter.

Find the right person to influence you.

When developing a profitable business-to-business marketing campaign on Instagram, selecting the appropriate influencer to work with is critical. You should search for influencers who have an audience that is similar to your target audience, who have a high engagement rate, and who are aligned with the values and messaging of your brand. Make use of platforms for influencer marketing in order to identify potential influencers and connect with them.

Determine what your objectives are.

In order to create a successful business-to-business marketing campaign with Instagram influencers, it is important to define your goals. Find out what it is you hope to accomplish through the collaboration, whether it be raising brand awareness, producing leads, or increasing sales. Make a plan for the campaign that is distinct and measurable by using this information.

Collaborate on content

When it comes to developing a successful business-to-business marketing campaign with Instagram influencers, content collaboration is an essential component. Collaborate with the influencer to produce content that is consistent with the messaging of your brand and that speaks directly to the members of your target audience. Make use of Instagram's features such as Stories, Live, and Reels to produce content that is both interesting and shareable.

Measure your results

When trying to determine whether or not your B2B marketing campaign with Instagram influencers was successful, it is essential to measure the results of your efforts. Track the engagement, reach, leads, and sales that were generated as a result of the collaboration using the analytics provided by Instagram as well as tools provided by third parties. Make use of this information to optimize the influencer marketing campaigns you will be running in the future.

Observe the rules set out by the FTC.

It is essential to conduct your B2B marketing campaign with Instagram influencers in accordance with the FTC's guidelines, as this will ensure compliance and transparency. Disclose the partnership in the content in a manner that is both clear and prominent, and use hashtags such as #ad and #sponsored where appropriate. It is important to provide the influencer with detailed instructions on how to disclose the partnership within their content.

Establish connections with people who have influence.

Establishing meaningful connections with Instagram's most influential users is critical to developing a B2B marketing strategy that is both effective and sustainable over the long term. Collaborate with influencers who have a genuine interest in your goods or services, as well as brand values and messaging that are congruent with those of your company. Maintaining these connections requires providing something of value to the influencer on a consistent basis and actively engaging in conversation with them.

Conclusion

Instagram influencers have the potential to be a powerful tool for B2B companies, allowing them to reach their target audience, increase brand awareness, and build credibility in their respective industries. Pick the right influencer for your campaign, be clear about your objectives, work together with other people to create content, track your progress, and evaluate your success while adhering to FTC guidelines. By adhering to these guidelines, you will be able to make the most of Instagram influencers in order to realize your B2B marketing objectives and expand your company's presence on the platform.

Chapter 25: A Guide to Creating Engaging Instagram Stories Ads

---

Using Instagram Stories Ads is a fantastic method for reaching your target demographic, promoting your goods or services, and driving sales on the Instagram platform. In this section, we will go over a guide for developing Instagram Stories Ads that are interesting to users.

Establish your goals and priorities.

Establishing your goals before beginning to create an Instagram Stories Ad is essential to achieving success. Find out what you want to accomplish with the Ad, such as increasing brand awareness, driving traffic to your website, or generating sales. Make a plan for the campaign that is distinct and measurable by using this information.

Make sure you use the correct format.

When developing an engaging Instagram Stories Ad, selecting the appropriate format is one of the most important steps. You have the option of selecting a variety of formats for your advertisements, such as single image or video Ads, carousel Ads, or full-screen Ads. Make use of captivating visuals and copy that speaks directly to your target audience and is in line with the messaging you want to convey about your brand.

Make use of Instagram's various artistic tools.

It is essential, when developing an engaging Instagram Stories Ad, to make use of the creative tools that Instagram provides. Create advertisements that are visually appealing and interactive by making use of features such as filters, stickers, and text overlays. Make your advertisement more engaging by adding a soundtrack from Instagram's music library and using it in it.

Make sure your call to action is compelling.

When it comes to increasing conversions from your Instagram Stories Ad, one of the most important things you can do is create an engaging call to action. Utilize language that is not only understandable but also actionable in order to encourage your target audience to take the action you want them to take, whether that action is visiting your website, making a purchase, or signing up for a newsletter.

Aim for the appropriate group of people.

It is important to target the appropriate audience in order to make sure that your Instagram Stories Ad is seen by the appropriate people. Utilize the targeting options provided by Instagram in order to communicate with users who fit a particular demographic, location, interest, or behavior. Retargeting customers who have already interacted with your brand on Instagram or your website can be accomplished with the help of custom audiences.

A/B testing and optimization of your ad

It is essential to test and improve the performance of your advertisement in order to achieve the goal you have set for yourself. Make use of Instagram's Ads Manager in order to monitor the level of engagement, reach, and conversions resulting from your advertisement. Make use of this information to improve the performance of your advertisement by modifying the targeting, creative, or call-to-action elements as necessary.

Conclusion

Through the use of Instagram Stories Ads, you can effectively reach your target audience, promote your products or services, and drive sales on the platform. Define your objective, select the appropriate format, make use of Instagram's creative tools, produce a call-to-action that is compelling, target the appropriate audience, and test and optimize your advertisement. If you follow these guidelines, you'll be able to produce engaging Instagram Stories Ads that help you meet your business objectives and expand your company's presence on the platform.

Chapter 26: How to Create Compelling Instagram Video Ads

───

Instagram Video Ads are an excellent tool for capturing the attention of your target audience, conveying the message you want to convey about your brand, and driving conversions on the platform. In the following section, we will go over the steps necessary to produce Instagram Video Ads that are compelling.

Establish your goals and priorities.

Establishing your goals before beginning to create an Instagram Video Ad is essential to achieving success. Find out what you want to accomplish with the Ad, such as increasing brand awareness, driving traffic to your website, or generating sales. Make a plan for the campaign that is distinct and measurable by using this information.

Make sure you pick the appropriate video format.

When developing an engaging Instagram Video Ad, selecting the appropriate video format is one of the most important steps. You have the option of selecting a variety of formats, such as full-screen ads, carousel ads, vertical videos, or square videos. Make use of visuals of a high quality and compelling copy that speaks to your target audience and aligns with the messaging you want to convey about your brand.

Keep it simple and to the point.

It is important to keep your Instagram Video Ad short and sweet if you want to capture the attention of your audience and drive engagement with your content. Employ messaging that is both clear and succinct in order to communicate the message of your brand to your audience while also offering them value. For the greatest possible impact, keep your video to under sixty seconds in length.

Use storytelling

Storytelling is an effective method for developing an emotional connection with an audience, which will in turn make your Instagram Video Ad more memorable to that audience. Make use of a story that is both compelling and relevant to the needs and interests of your target audience. Create a narrative that strikes a chord with your audience by incorporating visuals, music, and narration into your presentation.

Make sure your call to action is compelling.

When it comes to increasing conversions from your Instagram Video Ad, one of the most important things you can do is create an engaging call to action. Utilize language that is not only understandable but also actionable in order to encourage your target audience to take the action you want them to take, whether that action is visiting your website, making a purchase, or signing up for a newsletter.

A/B testing and optimization of your ad

It is essential to test and improve the performance of your advertisement in order to achieve the goal you have set for yourself. Make use of Instagram's Ads Manager in order to monitor the level of engagement, reach, and conversions resulting from your advertisement. Make use of this information to improve the performance of your advertisement by modifying the targeting, creative, or call-to-action elements as necessary.

Conclusion

The use of Instagram Video Ads is a potent method for attracting the attention of your target audience, conveying the message you want to convey about your brand, and driving conversions on the platform. Define your objective, select the appropriate video format, keep it brief and to the point, incorporate storytelling, develop an enticing call-to-action, and test and optimize your advertisement. If you follow these guidelines, you'll be able to produce compelling Instagram Video Ads that help you meet your business objectives and expand your company's presence on the platform.

Chapter 27: Optimizing Your Instagram Account for Search

———

The search function on Instagram is a powerful tool that can help you grow your business on the platform by reaching new audiences, attracting potential customers, and expanding your customer base. In this chapter, we'll go over how to optimize your Instagram account so that it can be found more easily in search results.

Use relevant keywords

It is essential to make use of relevant hashtags and keywords if you want to increase the discoverability of your Instagram account. Include in your bio, captions, and hashtags relevant keywords that reflect the messaging of your brand and the interests of your target audience. Make use of Instagram's search function to conduct research on pertinent keywords, then integrate the results of that research into your content strategy.

Complete your profile

It is important to fill out your profile completely in order to make a good first impression on potential customers who find you through a search. Make sure that your profile picture is crisp, professional, and reflects the identity of your brand. You should compose a bio that is succinct yet compelling; it should communicate your value proposition and encourage potential customers to learn more about your company. Utilize the features of your Instagram profile, such as highlights, to create a visually appealing and informative profile for your business and show off your products or services.

Use geotags

It is essential to make use of geotags if you want to increase the discoverability of your Instagram account in local searches. Make it easier for potential customers to find you in their area by including geotags in your posts and Stories. This will tag your location and make it clear where you are. Utilize the Explore feature on Instagram to conduct research on trending local hashtags, and then incorporate the results of that research into your content strategy.

Encourage engagement

It is important to encourage engagement on your Instagram account if you want to make it more visible in search results. Make use of copy and visuals that are interesting to the audience in order to encourage them to like, comment, and share your posts. Quickly respond to people's comments and direct messages, and maintain consistent interaction with the people who follow you. Make use of the engagement features offered by Instagram, such as polls, questions, and quizzes, to stimulate conversation and acquire a deeper understanding of your audience.

Join forces with those of other accounts.

When it comes to increasing your visibility in search results and expanding your reach to new audiences on the platform, collaborating with other accounts is essential. Collaborate with other accounts operating in the same market or specialization as you are in order to produce content that is of value to both of your audiences. Make use of the tagging feature on Instagram to increase the visibility of your posts by naming the account with which you are collaborating.

Use Instagram Ads

Increasing your visibility in search results and reaching new audiences are both important reasons to make use of Instagram Ads. Make use of Instagram's Ads Manager in order to create targeted advertisements that deliver the appropriate message to the appropriate audience. Make use of Instagram's conversion tracking feature to evaluate the efficacy of your advertisements and improve your overall performance.

Conclusion

It is essential to optimize your Instagram account for search if you want to expand your business on the platform, reach new audiences, and attract potential customers. Employ pertinent keywords, finish your profile, make use of geotags, encourage engagement, work together with other Instagram accounts, and make use of Instagram Ads. You will be able to optimize your Instagram account for search if you follow these tips, and you will also be able to accomplish your business goals on the platform.

Chapter 28: How to Run a Successful Instagram Contest

On Instagram, holding a contest is a fantastic way to boost engagement, expand your following, and broaden people's familiarity with your brand. In this chapter, we will go over the steps that need to be taken in order to successfully run a contest on Instagram.

Establish your goals and priorities.

Establishing your goals beforehand is an essential step in running a successful contest on Instagram. Determine the goals that you want to accomplish with the help of the contest, such as expanding your following, growing the number of people participating, or promoting a new product or service. Make use of this information to develop a contest strategy that is distinct and measurable.

Pick the appropriate kind of competition.

When designing an interesting and engaging Instagram contest, picking the appropriate contest type is critical. You have your choice of a variety of contest formats, such as "like to win," "comment to win," "tag a friend," and "user-generated content" competitions. Utilize a type of contest that complements your objective and provides value to the audience you are trying to reach.

Find out the regulations and requirements.

It is important to determine the rules and guidelines for your Instagram contest in order to guarantee that it will be held fairly and in accordance with Instagram's terms of service. Establish crystal-clear rules and regulations for the competition, including eligibility requirements, the length of the contest, entry methods, and specifics regarding the prizes. Create a landing page for the competition through the use of a third-party contest tool and supply all of the required information on that page.

Promote your contest

It is essential to promote your contest if you wish to reach your intended audience and increase the number of participants. You can promote the contest to both the audience you already have and to potential new followers by using the promotion features offered by Instagram, such as Stories, Reels, and Ads. When trying to reach a larger audience, it is helpful to make use of relevant hashtags and to work together with influencers or other brands.

Pick the appropriate amount of points.

Selecting the appropriate prize is essential to achieving your goals of encouraging participation and luring the people you want to see it. Choose a prize that fits in with the messaging of your brand as well as the interests of your target audience. Choose a prize that is both valuable and connected to your company's name, product, or service in some way.

Continue the discussion and make the winner public.

The importance of following up with your audience and announcing the winner cannot be overstated when it comes to creating a positive experience for them and maintaining their engagement. Keep in touch with all of the participants to express your gratitude for their involvement, and then make the winner's identity public. Make the announcement of the winner and highlight their submission by utilizing Instagram features such as Stories and Live.

Conclusion

Contests on Instagram are a powerful tool that can be used to increase engagement, grow your following, and build brand awareness on the platform. You should first determine your goal, then select the appropriate type of contest, then choose appropriate rules and guidelines, then promote your contest, select an appropriate prize, and finally follow up and announce the winner. You will be able to run a successful Instagram contest by following these tips, which will allow you to achieve your business goals and grow your business on the platform.

Chapter 29: Instagram and Crisis Management: A Guide for Damage Control

———

A crisis has the potential to be amplified on social media, which can have repercussions for a company's reputation. In this chapter, we will go over how to deal with a crisis on Instagram and how to use the platform to limit the amount of damage done.

Establish a strategy for dealing with emergency situations.

When it comes to effectively managing a crisis on Instagram, having a crisis management plan in place is an essential component. Make a plan that details the actions that need to be taken in the event of a crisis, such as determining the nature of the crisis, notifying key stakeholders, and formulating a response strategy. Establish a team or a single point of contact who is accountable for managing the situation on Instagram.

Listen in on what is being said.

Monitoring the conversation is essential for gaining a full comprehension of the magnitude of the crisis and formulating an appropriate response to it. Utilize social media listening tools in order to keep track of the conversation taking place on Instagram regarding the emergency. Keep an eye out for posts, hashtags, and comments that are connected to the emergency, and evaluate the overall tone of the discussion.

Quickly and accurately respond is expected.

When trying to manage a crisis on Instagram and minimize the damage it causes to your brand, it is important to respond as quickly and appropriately as possible. Quickly respond to questions, comments, and messages, and address concerns and inquiries in an open and honest manner. Maintain a tone that is open and compassionate while also accepting responsibility for any errors or problems that may occur.

Please keep me updated and provide information.

It is essential to keep your audience up to date with the latest information and updates in order to keep them informed about the crisis and the steps you are taking to resolve it. Make use of the Stories, Reels, and Live features offered by Instagram in order to provide timely and accurate information and updates to your audience. When communicating your response strategy and the steps to take next, make use of visuals and clear messaging.

Make amends and express your regret.

It is critical to demonstrate your dedication to your audience by offering an apology and working to rectify the situation in order to regain their trust in your brand. Make use of the tools provided by Instagram to publicly apologize, and then take the necessary steps to address the situation. You can demonstrate your dedication to making things right while also demonstrating your appreciation for customers who have been loyal to you by offering them incentives or promotions.

Gain wisdom from the past mistakes.

To avoid similar situations in the future and make your plan for managing crises more effective, it is essential to draw lessons from past experiences. Utilize the insights and analytics that Instagram provides in order to evaluate the impact of the crisis and locate areas that could use improvement. Put this experience to good use by developing some best practices and teaching your team how to handle a crisis.

Conclusion

The management of a crisis on Instagram can be difficult, but it also presents an opportunity to reestablish trust in your brand and demonstrate your dedication to the members of your audience. Establish a plan for handling a crisis, monitor the conversation, respond promptly and appropriately, provide updates and information, apologize and make things right, and draw lessons from the experience. If you follow these guidelines, you will be able to effectively manage a crisis on Instagram and use the platform to limit the extent of the damage.

Chapter 30: Conclusion: Mastering Instagram for Business Success

Instagram is a powerful platform that allows businesses to reach new audiences, build brand awareness, and drive conversions for their products and services. This book will guide you through a variety of topics to help you master Instagram for the purpose of achieving success in your business.

We began with an overview of the many reasons why Instagram is the most important platform for the success of businesses. We talked about the demographics of the platform's users, the engagement rates it sees, and the features that make it an effective tool for businesses.

Following that, we discussed a variety of topics, including how to craft the ideal Instagram profile, how to captivate your audience with captivating visuals and videos, how to use Instagram storytelling to build your brand, and how to establish goals and define your brand identity.

We also discussed how to build a loyal Instagram community through authenticity and connection, how to use Instagram insights to measure your success, and how to engage your followers through creative captions and hashtags.

We discussed more advanced topics such as the use of Instagram Live and IGTV for business purposes, as well as influencer marketing, partnering with other brands, advertising on Instagram, and more.

We also discussed topics that were unique to the various categories of businesses, such as developing a personal brand, utilizing Instagram for businesses that provide a service or have physical locations, as well as utilizing Instagram for businesses that are not-for-profit and B2B organizations.

In the end, we covered a variety of topics, including how to optimize your Instagram account for search, how to successfully run a contest on Instagram, and how to utilize Instagram for crisis management.

You will be able to master Instagram for your company's success and accomplish your goals on the platform if you follow the advice and strategies provided in this book. Don't forget to define your objectives, research your intended audience, craft content that will capture their attention, keep track of your progress, and continuously improve your strategy.

Because Instagram is always being updated with new features and trends, it is essential to keep abreast of these developments if one wishes to maintain a competitive edge on the platform. Make use of the resources that are provided by Instagram, go to seminars or conferences, and follow people who are considered to be leaders in their field.

Instagram has the potential to become a useful resource for the expansion of your company and the accomplishment of your objectives if you utilize it in the appropriate manner. If you can master Instagram, you can master the success of your business.

Also by B. Vincent

Affiliate Marketing
Affiliate Marketing
Affiliate Marketing

Standalone
Business Employee Discipline
Affiliate Recruiting
Business Layoffs & Firings
Business and Entrepreneur Guide
Business Remote Workforce
Career Transition
Project Management
Precision Targeting
Professional Development
Strategic Planning
Content Marketing
Imminent List Building
Getting Past GateKeepers
Banner Ads
Bookkeeping
Bridge Pages
Business Acquisition

Business Bogging
Business Communication Course
Marketing Automation
Better Meetings
Business Conflict Resolution
Business Culture Course
Conversion Optimization
Creative Solutions
Employee Recruitment
Startup Capital
Employee Incentives
Employee Mentoring
Followership
Servant Leadership
Human Resources
Team Building
Freelancing
Funnel Building
Geo Targeting
Goal Setting
Immanent List Building
Lead Generation
Leadership Course
Leadership Transition
Leadership vs Management
LinkedIn Ads
LinkedIn Marketing
Messenger Marketing
New Management
Newsfeed Ads
Search Ads
Online Learning
Sales Webinars

Side Hustles

Split Testing

Twitter Timeline Advertising

Earning Additional Income Through Side Hustles: Begin Earning Money Immediately

Making a Living Through Blogging: Earn Money Working From Home

Create Bonuses for Affiliate Marketing: Your Success Is Encompassed by Your Bonuses

Internet Marketing Success: The Most Effective Traffic-Driving Strategies

JV Recruiting: Joint Ventures Partnerships and Affiliates

Secrets to List Building

Step-by-Step Facebook Marketing: Discover How To Create A Strategy That Will Help You Grow Your Business

Banner Advertising: Traffic Can Be Boosted by Banner Ads

Affiliate Marketing

Improve Your Marketing Strategy with Internet Marketing

Outsourcing Helps You Save Time and Money

Choosing the Right Content and Marketing for Social Media

Make Products That Will Sell

Launching a Product for Affiliate Marketing

Pinterest as a Marketing Tool

Banner Blitz: Mastering the Art of Advertising with Eye-Catching Banners

Beyond Commissions: Maximizing Affiliate Profits with Creative Bonus Strategies

Retargeting Mastery: Winning Sales with Online Strategies

Power Partnerships: Mastering the Art of Business Growth Through Partnership Recruiting

The List Advantage: Unlocking the Power of List Building for Marketing Success

Capital Catalyst: The Essential Guide to Raising Funds for Your Business
Mobile Mastery: The Ultimate Guide to Successful Mobile Marketing Campaigns
Crowdfunding Secrets: A Comprehensive Guide to Successfully Funding Your Next Project
Insta-Success: Building Your Brand and Growing Your Business on Instagram

About the Publisher

Accepting manuscripts in the most categories. We love to help people get their words available to the world.

Revival Waves of Glory focus is to provide more options to be published. We do traditional paperbacks, hardcovers, audio books and ebooks all over the world. A traditional royalty-based publisher that offers self-publishing options, Revival Waves provides a very author friendly and transparent publishing process, with President Bill Vincent involved in the full process of your book. Send us your manuscript and we will contact you as soon as possible.

Contact: Bill Vincent at rwgpublishing@yahoo.com